This Notebook Belongs to:

Made in the USA
Middletown, DE
02 July 2022

68329840R00068